D0460815

ECONOMY

RENNAY CRAATS

Weigl Publishers Inc.

Published by Weigl Publishers Inc.
350 5th Avenue, Suite 3304, PMB 6G
New York, NY 10118-0069
Website: www.weigl.com

Library of Congress Cataloging-in-Publication Data

Craats, Rennay.
 Economy : USA past present future / Rennay Craats.
    p. cm.
 Includes index.
 ISBN 978-1-59036-980-7 (hard cover : alk. paper) -- ISBN 978-1-59036-981-4 (soft cover : alk. paper)
 1. United States--Economic conditions--Juvenile literature. 2. United States--Economic policy--Juvenile
literature. I. Title.
 HC103.C8777 2009
 330.973--dc22
                                    2008024084

Printed in the United States of America
1 2 3 4 5 6 7 8 9 0 12 11 10 09 08

All of the Internet URLs given in the book were valid at the time of publication. However, due to the
dynamic nature of the Internet, some addresses may have changed, or sites may have ceased to exist
since publication. While the author and publisher regret any inconvenience this may cause readers, no
responsibility for any such changes can be accepted by either the author or the publisher.

Weigl acknowledges Getty Images as its primary photo supplier for this title.

Every reasonable effort has been made to trace ownership and to obtain permission to reprint copyright
material. The publishers would be pleased to have any errors or omissions brought to their attention so
that they may be corrected in subsequent printings.

EDITOR: Heather C. Hudak
DESIGN: Terry Paulhus

Economy
Through The Years

Since the beginning of the 20th century, the U.S. economy has faced major challenges and achieved great successes. From the spending sprees of the the 1920s to the **Great Depression** of the 1930s, there have been extreme examples of "booms and busts" in the nation's financial history.

As the demand for certain products increase and supply diminishes, costs begin to skyrocket. Similarly, as products become more available, the price decreases, making it more affordable for the general public. In an effort to stabilize the economy, governments try to predict these trends.

The political climate of the entire world has an impact on the U.S. economy—what happens in other parts of the world can directly affect prices and events on home soil. The world wars overseas created a need for product rationing in the United States and required huge sums of money to fund. Importing and exporting products to and from other nations also contributes to the economic outlook of the United States.

Moving into the 21st century, the United States experienced some immediate economic challenges. As has always happened in the past, over time, the economy will shift, and these challenges will become opportunities.

5

2000s

Eco-cars Roll Out

Many people concerned about the environment believe that motor vehicles are one of the largest contributors to pollution and **global warming**. The gases given off by combustion engines stay in the atmosphere for a long time, trapping heat near Earth's surface. In response to customer concerns, car companies began to design more efficient vehicles. The results were called hybrid cars that used a combination of small gas engines and large batteries to move the car. Hybrid vehicles also used a technology known as regenerative braking. When a driver presses the brakes in a hybrid, the wheels become helped reduce the amount of gases given off by the engines and saved drivers a great deal of money on fuel. The first Hybrid sold in the United States was the Honda Insight in 1999, followed by the Toyota Prius in 2001. In 2007, Chevrolet announced that it had begun work on a new fuel-efficient vehicle, called the Volt, which will have an all-electric, zero-emission engine.

Eco-cars Roll Out

2001

The U.S. economy begins to decline, ending the longest period of constant growth in its history

2002

Wal-Mart becomes the largest corporation in the world, followed by General Motors and Exxon-Mobil

2001

Enron's End

Enron Corporation was one of the world's leading energy and utilities companies. In 2000, it claimed to have profits of $111 billion U.S. dollars. *Fortune Magazine* awarded Enron the title of "America's Most Innovative Company" multiple times. However, in 2001 most of Enron's success was revealed to be a fraud. The company had used forged reports to shareholders. Many Enron executives were charged with money laundering, fraud, insider trading, conspiracy, and other crimes. Chief Executive Officer Kenneth Lay was charged in 2004 with 11 offenses, after federal prosecutors spent years examining Enron's financial records. Lay was found guilty of 10 of these charges on May 5, 2006. He died of a heart attack while on vacation less than three months later. An **autopsy** revealed that Lay suffered from extensive heart disease which, by law, should have been reported to Enron shareholders. This was just one more detail that Lay had kept from his company's investors. Today, the corporation operates under the name of Enron Creditors Recovery Corporation. The current management hopes to recover all of the money lost by investors due to the widespread fraud that had been practiced under Lay.

2004

To Space, for a Price

In 2004, Sir Richard Branson of Virgin Group launched his Virgin Galactic division. Galactic is the first privately owned company to offer spaceflight to the public. Branson plans to base his "airline" on technology designed for SpaceShip One, the first privately owned vehicle to ascend to space. Virgin is widely known as a provider of luxury services, especially when it comes to their trans-Atlantic airline. At a price of $200,000 U.S. per ticket, few will be able to afford a trip into space. However, many economists suggest the price will decrease as the technology for private companies to reach space becomes more widely used and less expensive. The price of a ticket on a Virgin Galactic flight includes three days of astronaut training. Reservations for space flights opened in 2005, with actual flights scheduled to take in 2009.

Enron's End
Kenneth Lay

To Space, for a Price
Richard Branson

2003
U.S. interest rates reach their lowest point in 45 years

2004
The U.S. budget deficit is greater than $7 trillion

2005
The United States rejects the Kyoto Protocol, a treaty designed to reduce environmental harm

7

End of an Era
Alan Greenspan

Greenspan was able to stimulate growth in difficult times and prevent downturns in the economy from having a major impact on the lives of many U.S. citizens. Greenspan was well-respected and had a large following. Economists often made predictions based on his statements, so he often used neutral terms when sepaking about important economic matters. Greenspan wrote a memoir of his career in 2007, titled *The Age of Turbulence: Adventures in a New World*.

2008

Spending on Empty

In the early 21st century, many U.S. citizens borrowed money from credit companies and banks in order to buy expensive cars, vacations, and entertainment products, such as stereos and large televisions. As a result, many people received poor credit ratings and did not qualify for the assistance of their banks to purchase homes. **Subprime** lenders loaned money to people with poor credit—often at high rates of interest. In time, many of the people who had received subprime loans found they were unable to make payments. They either stopped paying or filed for bankruptcy. Banks began to **foreclose** on houses, leading to a downturn in the U.S. housing market. By 2008, houses in some neighborhoods were worth so much less than their original

2006

End of an Era

In 2006, one of the most important figures in U.S.

economics retired from public service. Alan Greenspan had been Chairman of the Board of Governors of the U.S. **Federal Reserve** Bank since his appointment by President Ronald Reagan in 1987. Shortly after taking over this position, Greenspan had to deal with the "Black Monday" stock market crash. Greenspan believed the powers of the Federal Reserve should only be used to intervene in the economy in times of crisis. By controlling interest rates,

2006	2007
Warren Buffet makes the largest charitable donation in history—$37 billion	The U.S. housing market falls 5.1 percent—its steepest drop in two decades

purchase price that they were abandoned by their owners. Many economists suggested that this was the first major sign of a coming **recession** in the U.S. economy.

Into the Future

Throughout history, the U.S. economy has faced many periods of extreme growth, as well as hard times. What can we learn from the past about economic trends? What factors have contributed to economic booms and recessions?

| 2008 | 2009 | 2010 |

Economy
1990s

Minimum Wage

$3.80. It increased again in 1991 to $4.25. Critics said that the increase would cause financial problems for small businesses, which would not be able to afford the higher wages. They claimed that it might cause people to lose their jobs. Despite these concerns, the minimum wage was raised to reflect **inflation** and the cost of living. However, the government recognized the concerns and said there could be a lower wage for training workers. These workers, who were often between the ages of 16 and 19, earned $3.61 per hour. This training wage would expire on March 31, 1993.

1990

Rebuilding the Economy

In 1990, President George H.W. Bush had the task of breathing life into a failing economy. The federal budget deficit had soared to $220 billion per year, which was three times what it was in 1980. The debt had swelled to $3.2 trillion, which was also three times that of 1980. The president tried to find common ground between the Democrats and the Republicans in Congress in order to establish a way to pay down the debt. Many Democrats thought that increasing taxes for wealthy people was the best solution. Republicans disagreed. They felt that federal spending cuts were the only way to cure the deficit problem. Congressional Democrats told Bush that he had to sign a

1990

Minimum Wage

In April 1990, the minimum wage for U.S. workers rose to

1991
Pan American World Airways claims bankruptcy.

1992
The U.S. economy begins to emerge from recession.

1993
IBM loses nearly $5 billion—the largest one-year loss for a corporation in U.S. history.

statement calling for tax revenue increases before there were any further discussions about the budget. Bush did not think this would go against his campaign promise of no new taxes. He was wrong. Republican supporters were angry. They pulled their support for the president and defeated the budget bill in the House of Representatives.

Balancing Act

President Clinton was dedicated to balancing the federal budget. With this promise came tax cuts for millions of people. The plan to balance the budget was the first of its kind since 1969. It stated that the federal deficit could be scrapped by 2002 if the U.S. economy stayed strong. A balanced budget came with a price. Clinton's bill called for government cuts. He expected to trim federal spending by $263 billion over five years. This included removing $140 billion from the government's compulsory programs, such as Medicare and Medicaid—the health programs for poor and elderly Americans. His bill also introduced $24 billion in new funding that would give uninsured children health coverage. Clinton left office before seeing if his plan would be a success.

Rebuilding the Economy
President George H.W. Bush

Balancing Act
President Bill Clinton, Newt Gingrich, and John Kasich

1994
Netscape goes public, inspiring a boom in NASDAQ, the technology market.

1995
The General Agreement on Tariffs and Trade becomes the World Trade Organization (WTO).

11

1992–1997

Downsizing

The word "downsizing" was used in the 1970s to refer to smaller homes and cars that people chose in order to combat high energy prices. By the 1990s, the term referred to reducing staff in companies. Between 1992 and 1997, 16.4 million Americans were victims of downsizing. At the same time, companies' profits and stock values rose. The heads of major corporations made higher salaries than CEOs anywhere else in the world, even when profits were stable or dropping. The message was clear—cutting jobs was a way to get ahead in business. Companies replaced their high-salaried American workers with those willing to work for much less and in countries with looser environmental and labor rules. While downsizing may have increased the bottom line, it did not necessarily make for an efficient workplace. People did not feel secure in their jobs. They knew they could be let go at any time, even if they were doing good work. The challenges and hardships associated with downsizing stayed with U.S. workers and families well past the nineties.

1993

Free Trade

President Bush wanted to boost U.S. trade. He suggested a North American Free Trade Agreement (NAFTA) as a way to do this. An agreement with Mexico and Canada would reduce or even remove trade tariffs on goods sold across the continent. Both Canada and Mexico were interested in the agreement and saw it as a way of helping North

1996

The stock market experiences exceptionally high gains after the presidential election

1997

McDonald's has 23,000 restaurants in 109 countries

1998

Internet companies, such as Yahoo!, Amazon, and Ebay, earn millions

12

Free Trade
President Bill Clinton

America compete with such areas as Asia and Europe, which already had free-trade zones. Bush's successor, Bill Clinton, carried on the agreement with Canadian Prime Minister Brian Mulroney and Mexican President Carlos Salinas de Gortari. NAFTA was passed by Congress in 1993 after a great deal of debate. It was put into effect in 1994. Many Americans and Canadians were afraid that companies would move their factories to Mexico to save money and that jobs would be lost as a result. Others were concerned that environmental regulations would be harder to enforce under NAFTA. Some of the concerns raised were dealt with in additional agreements in 1993 before NAFTA was approved.

Into the Future

What is the minimum wage in your city or town? What was it when your parents or grandparents were young? Why do you think it has increased so much over time? How much will you need to earn ten years from now to maintain your standard of living?

1999

Bill Gates, owner of software company Microsoft, becomes the world's richest man. He is worth $85 billion.

2000

President Bill Clinton announces the largest budget surplus in U.S. history.

because it had violated the rules against one company forming a monopoly. After a seven-year court battle, AT&T agreed to give up control of twenty-two regional telephone companies. It was able to keep Western Electric, its manufacturing business, and Bell Laboratories, its long-distance business. These components made the company the most money. After the settlement was reached, AT&T was able to enter the lucrative computer and electronics markets.

1980s

Good Intentions Gone Bad

Until the 1980s, the U.S. had a strong economy. The country had exported goods, ranging from clothes to metals, to the rest of the world. Due to an economic downswing, the U.S. had to buy many of these products from other countries in the eighties. To battle the recession, companies laid off employees and looked to the government for assistance. Americans experienced the first standard-of-living decline since World War II. The country's already high unemployment rate went higher. President Reagan promised to "put America back to work." He cut taxes and spending to help bring money into the U.S. The unemployment numbers dropped, and inflation remained steady. The economy began to grow after the slump

NOVEMBER 21, 1983 $1.75

TIME

MIDEAST
Tensions Keep
Rising

SPLITTING AT&T
Who Wins, Who Loses — And Why

Communication Breakdown

1982

Communication Breakdown

In 1982, communications giant AT&T agreed to break up into smaller companies. The government was concerned that the company had almost complete control of the telecommunications market. The Justice Department launched an **antitrust** lawsuit against AT&T

1981	1982	1983
President Reagan reduces marginal federal income taxes by 24 percent.	The world's largets company, AT&T, is broken into many smaller companies to dissolve its monopoly.	U.S. inflation rates drop to 3% per year.

14

in the early eighties, but the government tactics backfired. With the tax and spending cuts, there was not enough money coming in. The trade deficit grew from $19.7 billion to $119.8 billion between 1980 and 1989.

1980

Close Call for Chrysler

In January 1980, President Carter signed the Chrysler Loan Guarantee bill. This was a $1.5 billion bailout for the struggling automotive manufacturer. Chrysler was America's seventeenth-largest company and had lost $207 million in the last quarter of 1979. U.S. cars were not selling as well as reliable, gas-efficient Japanese cars. President Reagan later tried to restrict Japanese imports, but Japanese manufacturers built factories in the U.S. and continued to make cars.
To deal with this problem, Lee Iacocca, the tough chairman of Chrysler, set out to put the company on track. Many workers were laid off so the company could survive. In 1984, thanks to a turnaround plan, Chrysler posted a first-quarter profit of $705 million. The company had recovered from its tough time and paid off the government loan—seven years ahead of schedule. The government had made a profit of $350 million in interest.

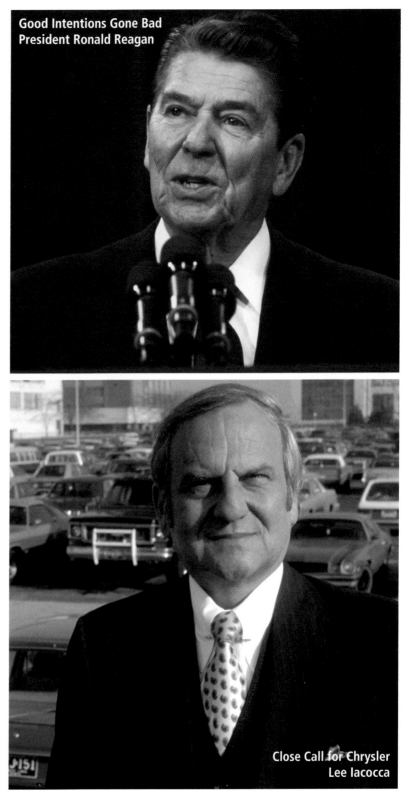

Good Intentions Gone Bad
President Ronald Reagan

Close Call for Chrysler
Lee Iacocca

1984

The Center for Japan-U.S. Business and Economic Studies is founded at New York University.

1985

The U.S. dollar declines in value compared to European and Japanese currencies.

Agriculture Buys the Farm

1987

Agriculture Buys the Farm

Tough times hit U.S. farmers in the 1980s. In 1987, prices for agricultural goods dropped, and interest rates soared. About 24,000 farmers were forced off their land. Banks foreclosed on farms that had been in families for generations. Independent farms were consolidated into huge agribusinesses. Also, since 1977, the percentage of farmers had dropped 9 percent of the U.S. population. This brought the number of people growing crops to the lowest level since the Civil War. Those farmers who kept their land struggled to make ends meet.

1986
The Tax Reform Act of 1986 is passed by U.S. Congress.

1987
Alan Greenspan is appointed chairman of the Federal Reserve Bank.

1988
In Washington, Missouri, Wal-Mart opens its first supercenter.

1987

Black Monday

On October 19, 1987, U.S. stock markets witnessed a plunge of 22 percent. This was almost double the fall of 1929, which set the Great Depression in motion. In one day, 604.5 million shares in companies were traded—more than double the previous record. The enormous drop cost stockholders around $500 billion. Many people lost everything they owned. Stock prices began to fall around the world. People waited nervously to see if this stock market crash, called Black Monday, would cause another economic depression. The Federal Reserve Bank took action. It put cash into the market, and banks started lending money again. Several companies began buying back their own stocks. These events, which happened within

Black Monday

a few days of the crash, helped the market recover. Confidence built again, and the market stabilized. Still, it took about

two years for the stock market to reach the level it was at before Black Monday.

Entire Store ON SALE

Everything Must Go!

Into the Future

During times of economic decline, businesses often find it hard to remain profitable. Think about the businesses in your community. When did they first open? Have any closed? What makes a business successful? Are there any businesses that would do especially well in your neighborhood?

1989
Business analyst Howard Dresner first uses the term "business intelligence."

1990
President Bush raises taxes to reduce the budget deficit.

17

Economy
1970s

Black Gold Rush

1970s

Black Gold Rush

In the 1970s, people discovered the economic impact of oil. Those who had oil had power. Those who did not, needed it. The U.S. claimed only around 6 percent of the world's population, but it used one-third of the energy resources. This became a problem in 1973. The Organization of Petroleum Exporting Countries (OPEC) raised the price of oil by nearly 200 percent within a few months. It put a similar **embargo** in place against any other country that supported Israel. OPEC members included Iran, Kuwait, Saudi Arabia, and Qatar. Much of the world experienced an energy crisis. In an effort to conserve energy, President Nixon tried to reduce highway speed limits to 50 miles per hour. The embargo was lifted in 1974 after the U.S. helped establish a ceasefire in the **October War**. The crisis showed the world that the new economic powers were countries with oil wells.

1970s

Economic Turbulence

In the 1970s, the U.S. faced several economic challenges. The trade deficit soared, while gold reserves shrank. Inflation and unemployment rates skyrocketed. To try to prevent a serious problem, President Nixon stopped gold payments in 1971. Unbacked by gold, the U.S. dollar had to re-establish itself against other currencies in the world. Many other countries that put their money up against the U.S. dollar could no longer do so. No country's money had a fixed value compared to another. The dollar fell in comparison to the Japanese yen and West German mark. In December

Deep Freeze
President Richard Nixon

1971, ten of the world's leading non-communist countries met to end the money crisis. After the meeting of the Group of Ten, a system of controlled rates was introduced into international commerce policy.

1971

Deep Freeze

In 1971, President Nixon took the gloves off in his fight against inflation. For three months, he froze wages and prices. This meant that salary and price increases were not allowed. After the three-month period, the freeze began to thaw slightly. Nixon introduced a one-year time frame during which wages and prices could rise again, but not by very much. Prices were allowed to go up only enough to cover costs but not to increase profits. Workers were not allowed raises in pay that covered past work. Wages could increase by no more than 6.6 percent each year. Nixon continued to fight inflation until his resignation in 1974.

1973
Motorola's Martin Cooper invents the first cellular telephone

1974
President Ford makes the Whip Inflation Now speech

1975
In the United States, the average cost of 1 gallon of gas is 57 cents

19

Bailing Out the Big Apple
President Gerald Ford

permitting the Federal Treasury to lend $2.3 billion to the city each year for three years. This bailout was aimed at helping New York cover its monthly debt payments of nearly $1 billion. Ford insisted that part of the loan be paid back every year. Some taxpayers argued that the government should not have stepped in. They thought it was a drain on tax money.

1976

Tough Times

In 1976, the U.S. unemployment rate went through the roof. It rose for three months in a row, and an estimated 25.9 million U.S. people were living in poverty. This was the largest number since 1970. Then, in 1979, inflation hit a high all over the world. People made less money but continued to spend. As a result, more money circulated, and the inflation rate rose. The inflation rate reached 172 percent in Argentina, and the rate hit double digits in

1975

Bailing Out the Big Apple

In 1975, New York City was on the verge of bankruptcy, and people were looking to the federal government for help. President Ford announced that he would block Congress's attempt to arrange a loan. The next day, a *New York Times* headline read "Ford to City: Drop Dead." The pressure that resulted caused Ford to change his mind. Many people feared

that a financial collapse in New York City would cause serious problems in worldwide banking. Ford finally agreed to help the New York City government stay afloat. The huge city was about to **default** on loans, so President Ford signed legislation

Tough Times

1976	1977	1978
The average cost of a new house in the United States is $48,000.	The U.S. Department of Energy is formed.	Voters approve Proposition 13, lowering California property taxes by nearly 60 percent.

France and Great Britain. It neared 15 percent in the U.S. The skyrocketing prices for oil and gas as a result of the OPEC crisis added fuel to the fire. For Americans, the seventies ended with a nervous eye toward the economy.

1977

Black Alaskan Gold

After three years of construction, an enormous oil pipeline was at last finished. In June 1977, oil began flowing through the Alaska pipeline to the rest of the country. The lines ran from Prudhoe Bay's North Slope oil fields to refineries in Valdez on Prince William Sound. This Alaskan oil reserve was one of North America's richest supplies. More than $9 billion had been spent setting up the pipelines. They were built to pump 2 million barrels of petroleum out of the oilfield each day. The more than 800 miles of pipe crossed

Black Alaskan Gold

800 rivers. The first oil piped through the pipeline reached refineries on July 28. The oil drawn from this field allowed the U.S. to reduce imports from the Middle East and other oil-rich regions by 15 percent.

Into the Future

In the 1970s, the price of oil skyrocketed, causing many people to look for less expensive modes of transportation and more efficient ways to heat their homes. Look at energy costs today. Are they more affordable than in the 1970s? Do people still look for more affordable ways to acquire energy? Why?

1979

1980

Economy
1960s

The New Frontier
President John F. Kennedy

Boosting the Economy

1960s

The New Frontier

President John F. Kennedy spoke about the New Frontier. His plan was to create a steady and high rate of economic growth in the U.S. He asked for medical coverage for senior citizens, more money set aside for education, the responsible use of natural resources, and housing and community development. While some of his economic efforts failed, he fought for others and won. He raised the national minimum wage from $1.00 to $1.25 over four years. He also increased the number of workers affected by the legislation by 3.5 million. President Kennedy promised to cut tariffs by 50 percent over a 5-year period and to get rid of the tax altogether on some items. This policy was prompted by the quickly developing European Union. The U.S. had to remain competitive in trade, and the lifted taxes allowed the U.S. to trade freely with countries in Europe.

1960s

Boosting the Economy

President Kennedy tried to jump-start the economy in the early 1960s. In 1962, prices on the New York Stock Exchange dropped dramatically. It was the

1961
U.S. Congress passes the Foreign Assistance Act.

1962
The United States spends 9.3 percent of its gross domestic product on defense.

1963
President Kennedy issues the Cuban Assets Control Regulations.

sharpest decline since the 1929 market crash that had started the Great Depression. Kennedy began taking measures to help businesses prosper. By 1963, he had proposed an enormous tax cut. He wanted to slash taxes by more than $10 billion, which also included lowering business taxes. He wanted people to feel confident in the economy and keep spending money. If they were taxed less, citizens would have more to spend. An increased minimum wage was geared at giving Americans a bit more cash in their pockets. The extra spending would then encourage new businesses, and the taxes brought in from the expanded economy would make up for the loss from the initial cut. Many Americans supported these efforts, but some still insisted that the government was anti-business, especially after Kennedy's hard line with the steel industry.

1964
Cable TV hits the airways in the United States.

1965
The Canada–United States Automotive Agreement is signed.

1962

Steel Stress

In his first year as president, John F. Kennedy took part in negotiations between major steel companies and their workers. Kennedy wanted to keep labor costs down so that the companies could keep their prices at a steady level. By the end of 1962, the parties decided that workers' wages would remain the same but that their benefits would be increased. With this deal, Kennedy assumed that steel companies would not raise their prices. He was wrong. Two weeks later, the president of U.S. Steel announced a price increase of $6 per ton. Kennedy viewed this as a betrayal. He attacked the action and launched a grand jury investigation on price fixing in the steel business. Three days later, several steel companies reduced their prices. By April 14, U.S. Steel had reduced its prices, too. While Kennedy came out on top, the situation hurt relationships between the government and businesses. Kennedy's battle against the steel companies confirmed American businesspeople's view that Kennedy and the Democrats were not friendly toward big business. Kennedy's hard work during the previous year to convince people otherwise was wasted.

1966

In the United States, a first-class stamp costs 5 cents.

1967

The average annual household income in the United States is $33,338.

1968

The Intel Corporation is founded to manufacture microchips.

War on Poverty

In 1964, President Johnson declared war on poverty in the U.S. His economic program called for a system to help people in areas of extreme poverty. This system included such safety nets as greater access to food stamps and unemployment payments. Johnson called for a youth program that would help get young Americans into the workforce—part of the "job corps." There needed to be special assistance to schools, libraries, hospitals, and nursing homes so that all Americans would be part of the solution. Johnson asked Congress for $962 million to put his plan to fight poverty into action. At the same time, he began cutting in other areas, including the Defense Department and

War on Poverty
President Lyndon B. Johnson

Atomic Energy Commission projects. He managed to trim about $2 billion, which enabled him to add small amounts to his

poverty program. This was one war the U.S. public could get behind.

Into the Future

Having a healthy economy involves more than just earning high wages. Funding from governments and donors for services, such libraries, hospitals, and schools, contributes to a healthy economy. Think about your community. What services are funded through donors or the government? Would you be willing to pay for these services if funding was no longer available? What other services would you like to have in your community?

1969

The computer network ArpaNET, which would eventually become the Internet, is created

1970

Santa Clara Valley, California, is home to five of the seven largest semiconductor producers in the United States

Economy
1950s

1952

Nerves of Steel

After World War II, the U.S. experienced a period of severe economic inflation. This caused workers to go on strike in many major industries. President Truman knew that, of all the industries, he could not afford to allow a steel strike. The war effort in Korea depended on steel production. Steelworkers had been working without a contract since the beginning of the year, and a strike date had been set for April 9, 1952. Hours before the strike was to begin, Truman took action. He ordered Secretary of Commerce Charles Sawyer to take control of the steel mills in order to ensure that war production continued. This was only a temporary solution. The Supreme Court ruled against the president's seizure, saying it was unconstitutional. After the verdict, the planned steel strike was carried out. Steelworkers left the factories and stayed off the job for fifty-three days until an agreement was reached. Another steel strike hit in 1959. The Supreme Court ordered workers back to work, and President Eisenhower reminded both sides of their obligation to resolve the issues. The strike had lasted 116 days—the longest steel strike to date.

1953

The Rise and Fall of Eisenhower's Economy

President Eisenhower was a firm believer that local, not federal, governments should have control over their own affairs. He reduced taxes and called for cuts in federal spending in an attempt to balance the budget. He also removed wage and price controls to let the economy flourish on its own. At the same time, he expanded Social Security benefits and created a new department to handle health, education, and welfare. In the fifties, Americans were hit with rising living costs, budget deficits, and lower agricultural prices. In 1953, a nearly two-year economic recession swept the country. The slump was ended by the Revenue Act of 1954. This cut taxes and relaxed credit. President Eisenhower also

Nerves of Steel

1951
Long Island banker William Boyle creates the Franklin Charge Account Plan, paving the way for credit cards.

1952
The United States produces 73 percent of the world's cars.

increased federal spending on roadways and schools. The economy rebounded and slowly began to grow again.

1955

Union Power

A huge union superpower took shape in December 1955. The deal was pushed through by George Meany, a strong union man from the pre-Depression days. The American Federation of Labor (AFL) united with the Congress of Industrial Organizations (CIO). Together, these organizations represented about 16 million U.S. union members. The merger had been in the works since 1952. Dwight Eisenhower had become the first Republican president in 20 years. Labor unions had traditionally backed Democratic candidates, whom they trusted to look after their needs. This change in leadership heightened the labor unions' feeling that a united front was needed in dealing with the government. George Meany was elected president of the AFL-CIO and served in that position for 25 years. During his run, he expelled the Teamsters Union from the organization. The Teamsters was the most powerful and largest union since the war, and it was kicked out of the AFL-CIO for corruption in 1957. It took thirty years for the union to shake off its shady reputation and disreputable leaders and be allowed back into the AFL-CIO.

The Rise and Fall of Eisenhower's Economy
President Dwight Eisenhower

Union Power

Friedman's Philosophy
Milton Friedman

1957

Friedman's Philosophy

Economist Milton Friedman fought the U.S. government's economic position. In 1957, his book *A Theory of the Consumption Function*, criticized Western economic policies after World War II. Friedman and his associates—called the "Chicago School" for their connection to the University of Chicago—wanted to put **monetarism** back into practice. They argued that money supply and interest rates were the keys to economic growth, not government spending and taxation. Friedman's theory held that the demand for money and the speed at which it circulated in society were constant. He argued against the belief that money demand depended on the interest rates. If money is circulated at fixed rates rather than with a changing interest rate, economic stability could be achieved. Friedman's ideas were left out of economic policies for two decades. By the 1980s, presidents and prime ministers around the world were looking at his theories when trying to improve their countries' economies.

1956
The first Japanese car is sold in the United States

1957
The S&P 500 is developed to assess the stock market as a whole

1958
A worldwide recession takes place

Hard Times

Late 1950s

Hard Times

In the late 1950s, Americans experienced some hard times. Stock prices began to **fluctuate** in 1957, beginning a 9-month economic slump. This came after several years of unheard-of prosperity across the nation. At the beginning of 1958, a recession swept the country. By the middle of the year, the economy had grown even worse. Unemployment rates skyrocketed. More than 5 million Americans were without jobs in June. This was the highest level of unemployment since World War II. By the end of the year, the downturn had been stabilized, and the economy set out on a slow road to recovery.

Into the Future

Events that take place overseas, such as the Korean War, often have a direct effect on the U.S. economy. If there is a war in oil-rich countries, your parents may pay more to fill their car with fuel. Poor weather in China may harm rice crops, raising the price you pay for this staple food. Think about events taking place around the world today. Do they affect the economy where you live? How?

1959

Cuba passes the

1960

Venezuela, a major oil-producing nation in South America

Economy
1940s

Battling Inflation

Battling Inflation

America did not fall into a depression after the war as many predicted. This was partly due to the high demand for goods that people had gone without in the war years. The real threat was inflation. The nation was reeling under wage and price controls. Business managers beat the system on the black markets. Workers fought against controls by striking. President Truman tried to stabilize the economy. He asked for permission to draft strikers into the army. The Senate rejected this request. Congress then enlarged the Office of Price Administration, but its authority was so diluted that Truman **vetoed** the move. In July 1946, there were no price or wage controls in the country. Prices soared by more than 25 percent. Congress moved quickly to pass another bill restricting this freedom, but the damage to consumers' pocketbooks was done. Luckily, supply soon caught up with demand. The average inflation rate without controls settled at around 6 percent. President Truman continued his fight to rebuild the economy after being re-elected in 1948.

1941
The attack on Pearl Harbor takes place, spurring the United States to join World War II.

1942
The Alaska Highway opens.

1943
President Roosevelt signs a "hold-the-line order," freezing wages and jobs.

1940s

Money Troubles

During the war years, Roosevelt's government spent more than $320 billion. Taxation brought about $130 billion into the wartime economy. The rest of the money came from borrowing from other countries. In 1944 alone, the government created a debt of more than $50 billion—more than twice the country's total debt in 1941. By the end of the war, the debt had ballooned to about $280 billion. This was almost six times larger than when Pearl Harbor was attacked. With the fighting over, the government had to find a way to reduce the debt, provide jobs, and rebuild after the massive spending of the previous years.

1944
The United Nations Monetary and Financial Conference takes place in Bretton Woods, New Hampshire.

1945
The United Nations officially forms.

Truman's New Deal

President Truman had a Democratic Congress, but his **Fair Deal** program was met with resistance. Congress approved some of Truman's proposals but rejected others. The public housing bill, increased social security coverage, and higher minimum wage were approved by Congress. So were the Fair Deal's proposals for more subsidies for farmers, flood control, and **rural electrification**. Congress opposed Truman's proposals to construct the St. Lawrence Seaway and create several public hydroelectric companies. Congress also rejected Truman's civil rights proposals, which included an anti-**lynching** law. Truman was disappointed by the rejection, but he was not discouraged. He strengthened civil rights through his actions with the Justice Department, and he appointed African Americans to high offices.

1946

Workers on Strike

The war overseas was over, but there was a war at home to fight. Industries had made a great deal of money from the war. After the war, many workers were laid off. Because

Workers on Strike

of this and other reasons, 4.5 million workers went on strike in 1946. This brought the coal, steel, automobile, and electric industries to their knees. There were about 113 million worker-days lost due to the striking. Still, the strikers brought with them new peace, and the strikes were nonviolent.

1941

War Production

In 1941, only 15 percent of U.S. industry was producing military items. Military spending was about $2 billion per month. By the early to mid-1940s, much of the economy was focused on the war. Many companies stopped business as usual and began producing materials needed to fight the war in Europe. President Roosevelt set high quotas to be met for 1942. He wanted 60,000 planes, 45,000 tanks, and 20,000 anti-aircraft guns. In the first six months of 1942, the government spent more than $100 billion on war contracts. There were

Truman's New Deal
President Harry Truman

1946
George Marshall develops a plan to aid the econonomic recovery of Europe from World War II.

1947
The General Agreement on Tariffs and Trade (GATT) is created.

more goods on order than the economy had ever produced in one year. Now, about 33 percent of the economy was devoted to military production. The U.S. had a huge store of weapons and army vehicles. Toward the end of the war, defense plants were told to stop producing items such as anti-tank guns and trainer planes. Despite the large number of war products made in the U.S. during World War II, they accounted for only 40 percent of the gross national product.

Into the Future

World War II had a huge impact on economies around the world, including the United States. How did the country pay for its war efforts and help fund recovery programs in other parts of the world? Today, wars continue to take place around the world. What aid, if any, does the United States provide to these events?

1948
U.S. Congress passes the Economic Cooperation Act.

1949
The Point Four Program is introduced.

1950
The Diner's Card, the first credit card, is introduced to U.S. consumers.

Economy
1930s

Smoot-Hawley No Help

The Smoot-Hawley Tariff was supposed to ease the effects of the Depression on Americans.

Instead, it made the situation worse and helped the disaster spread across the world. The 1930 law allowed for an increase on tariffs of imported goods from 33 percent to 40 percent. This was the highest

the tariffs had ever been. Economists were afraid that this measure would hurt the country's international trade and asked President Hoover to reject the bill. Hoover refused. He wanted to protect U.S. companies, which were already in trouble after the stock market crash, from foreign competition. The economists were right. Between 1930 and 1932, unemployment in the

Smoot-Hawley No Help

1931

More than 800 U.S. banks close between September and October.

1932

The last steam-powered automobile is built.

34

U.S. soared from 3 million to 13 million, and there were 30 million unemployed people in the industrialized world. World trade plummeted from $2.9 billion a month to less than $1 billion by 1933. The loss of the U.S. as a trading partner caused hardships in nearly every country except the Soviet Union. The Smoot-Hawley Tariff had not helped—it contributed to the terrible economic disaster felt throughout the thirties.

1932

Legal Protection for Workers

The thirties were plagued by union issues. Many workers wanted unions, and many employers did not. In 1932, Congress passed the Norris-La Guardia Act. The new law was only one of many steps. Union membership had dropped drastically since the stock market crash, and wages were lower as well. Unemployment skyrocketed to more than 10 million. Regardless, the law was seen as a step in the right direction. It stated that business owners could not deny employment to workers who wished to join a union. The Act also recognized workers' right to "association and self-organization"—in other words, the right to have unions. Labor leaders were excited by the new law. They hoped it would encourage disgruntled workers and strengthen the economy at the same time.

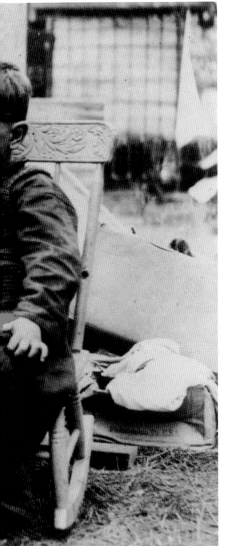

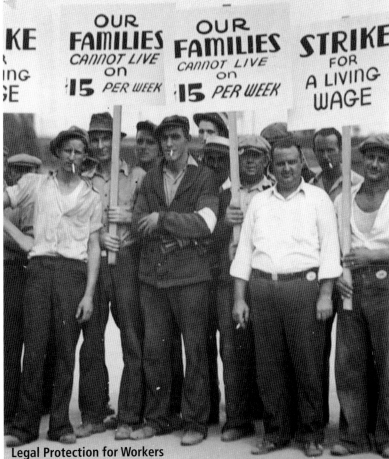

Legal Protection for Workers

1933
Prohibition, a law banning the sale of alcohol, is repealed.

1934
The Securities and Exchange Commission is created.

1935
The creation of nylon leads to a decline in cotton production.

Lean Years

The stock market crash of 1929 had devastated the economy in many countries of the world. People were ruined and did not know what to do. In 1931, 20,000 people committed suicide because they could not handle the Depression. This number was even greater than the record numbers of suicides immediately after the crash. Then, on March 4, 1933, the U.S. banking system collapsed.

It came on the last day of President Hoover's term in office. He had been blamed for the desperate situation in which the U.S. found itself. Some white-collar Americans lost everything because the banks collapsed. To make matters worse, the amount of industrial production in 1933 was less than half what it had been before the crash. Between 13 and 15 million Americans—one-quarter of the workforce—could not find jobs and struggled to care for their 30 million dependents. Poverty had struck about 40

million Americans by the time the Depression was over. Men and women stood in long lines at soup kitchens for a piece of bread or watery soup. Others searched through garbage on the street in hopes of finding a morsel to eat. Those fortunate enough to find jobs earned little, as wages dropped 40 to 60 percent. Farmers tried to stay afloat in the face of low prices for wheat, milk, and cotton. As President Franklin D. Roosevelt entered office, Americans hoped for better times with a new president.

Lean Years

1936	1937	1938
Keynesian economic practices make their debut in the United States.	The zeppelin industry fails after the Hindenburg crash in New Jersey.	Hewlett-Packard is founded.

Making Work

President Roosevelt wanted to create jobs and kick-start the economy. In 1933, he introduced the Public Works Administration (PWA), established under the National Industrial Recovery Act as the Federal Emergency Relief Administration. This organization brought masses of workers together across the country to build such public works as water supply systems, flood control systems, roads and bridges, and ports. From its beginning until 1939, PWA pumped more than $6 billion and 4.75 billion work hours of labor into building projects. They included about 35 percent of all new hospitals and health agencies; 65 percent of sewage plants, city halls, and courts; 70 percent of all schools; and 10 percent of all new transportation facilities in the nation. While PWA financed these projects,

Making Work

the new Works Progress Administration (WPA) over saw the work. It also recruited artists, writers, and performers. By finding them work, it became a major supporter of the arts.

Into the Future

During the Great Depression, many items that people use daily were difficult to acquire. Food and clothing were rationed, and jobs were hard to find. What would it be like to live during this time? How is this different from today?

CARS & TRU
JOB OPPORTUNITIES
REAL STATE

1939

Pan American Airlines begins to offer the world's first transatlantic passenger flights.

1940

The Jeep is invented. It sees heavy production and use by the U.S. military.

Real Estate Booms

1921

Real Estate Booms

Not since the Wild West of the 1800s had there been such a land boom. Tens of thousands of people rushed to Florida to get in on the action. They were eager to buy pieces of the state that had been advertised as paradise. The warm climate and the idea of an American Riveria like the one in France attracted investors by the hundred. Many buyers agreed to purchase land without seeing it first. They often discovered too late that they were the new owners of swampland. The land boom in Florida was at its height in 1925. A devastating hurricane in 1926 brought it to an abrupt end, destroying developments and the railroad to Key West.

1921

Americans buy 43 billion cigarettes.

1922

60,000 radios can be found in American homes.

The Roaring Twenties

1922

The Roaring Twenties

The twenties really began to roar in 1923. The recession experienced after World War I was over. Stock market values hit the roof. The gross national product was up 14 percent from 1922, and only 2.4 percent of the population was unemployed. Americans were encouraged to spend their new-found wealth on themselves. Mass-produced cars, cosmetics, and clothing were trumpeted as must-haves. After the horrors of war, Americans wanted to have fun, and they spent their money on products that helped them achieve that goal. Now that they had shorter workweeks, there was more time to spend on leisure activities with family and friends. People across the country were eager to live life to the fullest.

1923
Roy and Walt Disney found
The Walt Disney Company.

1924
Thomas Watson founds
the IBM Corporation.

1925
It costs $290 to buy
a Model T Ford.

The Good Times Roll

Mellon Axes Taxes
Andrew W. Mellon

1923

The Good Times Roll

President Coolidge's policies had helped the economy. People across the country were working, except in a few industries, such as coal and textiles. By 1923, industrial workers were earning twice what they had in 1914. Their wages continued to climb until 1928. By then, wages across the board were about one-third higher than they had been in 1923. This was partly because cheap energy kept manufacturing and shipping costs low. As well, employers thought that offering higher wages would prevent their workers from wanting to join labor unions. Since Americans were earning decent wages, they spent more money and bought more goods. This helped the manufacturers and storekeepers. The price of food fell, as did goods manufactured in industries that were mechanized. As a result, earnings could buy even more goods than before. Americans continued to make and spend money until the stock market crash in 1929.

1926

Mellon Axes Taxes

Treasury secretary Andrew W. Mellon, one of the country's richest men, believed that low taxes fueled the economy. He lobbied Congress for huge cuts in corporate and income taxes. The result was the 1926 Revenue Act. Mellon thought that these cuts would help all Americans, but it was wealthy Americans who benefited most. Still, the tax cuts did help the country as a whole because wealthy people had more money to put back into the economy. This extra money in the stock market and in society fueled the boom of the twenties. This boom ended with a crash when the stock market plummeted in 1929.

1926	1927	1928
Alan Greenspan is born on March 6.	GM sells more than one million cars, pulling ahead of Ford.	The Galvin Manufacturing Corporation, later known as Motorola, is founded.

All Good Things...

It seemed as though the good times and good fortune of the twenties would never end, but they did. The economic boom fizzled quickly on October 24, 1929 with the New York Stock Exchange crash. Thousands of Americans lost everything they owned. By the end of the day, the pressure and stress pushed eleven financiers to commit suicide. The day became known as Black Thursday. Although there were some warning signs, the financial bust came as a surprise to most Americans. Since 1925, the stock prices had more than doubled, and the Dow Jones, which measured the value of major stocks, had reached record highs. At the same time, the world economy was slowing, and stocks were very overpriced. Many investors listened to these warnings and cashed in their shares. As more people pulled out of the market, the stock prices dropped. On October 19, Americans across the country scrambled to dump their stocks. For five days, investors sold, and prices

All Good Things...

plummeted. Then, the bottom fell out of the stock market, and panic swept the country. Many companies went out of business. Those who survived cut back on production and employees. Millions of people were out of work. Wages and prices fell, and people bought only essential goods. Banks demanded loan and mortgage paybacks. Thousands of people were ruined. The government thought the system would correct itself, so it did little to help. By 1933, unemployment skyrocketed, people were hungry, and there was no end in sight. The Great Depression lasted until the late 1930s.

Into the Future

After World War I, the U.S. economy soared. Many people had plenty of money to spend and were eager to buy new products. Imagine that you have an unlimited money supply. What would you buy? How would you help others?

1929
The stock market crash on October 24 becomes known as Black Thursday.

1930
Following the stock market crash, the Sears Catalogue states, "thrift is the spirit of the day."

41

Economy
1910s

Striking Out

union were beaten or even lynched. The path toward reform was slow and difficult, but the strikers' actions helped lay the groundwork for future labor legislation in the U.S.

Rolling Down the Line

Automobile makers, such as the Ford Motor Company, produced 160,000 cars per year. In 1913, Henry Ford tried something new at his Highland Park, Michigan plant. He introduced the assembly line, which was based on the process lines of Singer sewing machine and Colt firearms plants. Ford's assembly line was a bit different. Unlike process lines, Ford's conveyor belt did not wait for a whole process to be completed. Instead, workers performed the same, small task on the line as the automobile part passed by. Employees had to work quickly and could not rest, or the piece would pass before they had done the necessary task. Ford's new system made skilled workers unnecessary. Before, a skilled worker had completed a single magneto wheel in twenty minutes. Now, twenty-nine unskilled workers finished the same job in thirteen minutes—each employee turned a screw or made an adjustment as the wheel rolled down the line. The time was later decreased to five minutes. The assembly line brought about the eight-hour shift and a five-dollar day. This

1910s

Striking Out

As many as one-half of U.S. laborers worked twelve-hour days often seven days a week. They were paid very little for their efforts. Many people lived in slums near the factories at which they spent most of their time. They wanted a six-day workweek and better working conditions. In the 1910s, workers began to take steps toward labor reform, and strikes and unrest swept the country. Large companies were threatened by the strikers' demands. The companies felt their property rights were at risk. As a result, strikers were met with violent company guards, brutal strikebreakers, and, at times, police forces that sympathized with the companies. In

Colorado, 9,000 striking coal miners stayed off the job for more than a year and a half. In 1914, a group of company guards attacked the strikers' camp armed with guns. They killed at least twenty-one people and injured one hundred. From January to June 1916, there were more than 2,000 strikes and lockouts. In 1917, striking members of the Industrial Workers of the World, a radical union, were taken from their beds at gunpoint, forced into trucks, and dumped in a New Mexican desert with minimal food and water. They were later imprisoned until the strike was broken. Other members of this

1911
Rockefeller's Standard Oil is broken up by new anti-trust laws.

1914
Ford's share of the U.S. auto market is 48 percent.

1915
Financial management company Merrill Lynch is founded.

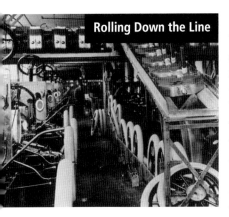
Rolling Down the Line

was double the average wage before the assembly line. The company could afford such wages because it was making so many cars. Once Ford's assembly line was perfected, one Model T was rolling off the line every twenty-four seconds. This allowed for an incredible increase in production. It also brought car prices down. Model Ts dropped from $850 in 1908 to $440 in 1914.

1913

Tariff Relief

One of President Wilson's top priorities was to lower tariff rates. He wanted to break down monopolies that were protected by the high tax that other countries had to pay when importing goods into the U.S. He wanted to prevent U.S. companies from charging high prices because there was no competition. Wilson did not want to wait for these reforms, so he pushed the bill forward quickly. The Underwood Tariff was prepared and ready for the president's signature by October

1913. This bill cut taxes on imported, manufactured, and semi-manufactured goods. The average tariff dropped from 41 to 27 percent. In addition, the bill got rid of taxes on most raw materials. For instance, the import tax on sugar was eventually removed. This was the first time that tariffs had been reduced since before the Civil War. Wilson's bill also provided for a tax on income to replace some of the money lost due to lower tariffs. World War I slowed

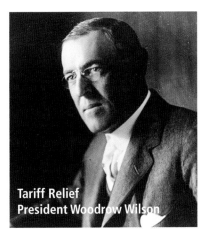
Tariff Relief
President Woodrow Wilson

U.S. trade with other countries. The issue of tariffs did not become a hot topic again until the economic slump of 1920 and 1921. At that time, customs taxes were increased to levels higher than had ever been seen before.

1914

Fair Practice

The government stepped into business in 1914 by establishing the Federal Trade Commission

Fair Practice

UNITED STATES

FEDERAL TRADE COMMISSION BUILDING

(FTC). This independent body replaced the Bureau of Corporations. Members of the Commission were appointed by the president with Senate approval. To ensure fairness, no more than three of the five members could be from the same political party. The FTC set out to make sure that business practices were fair in order to protect the interests of everyday Americans. The commission targeted such offenses as price-fixing, misleading advertising, false labeling of products, unfair competition, and poor quality products. Its job was to make sure that Americans could make choices based on facts. If a business was guilty of engaging in any these practices, the commission could order it to stop doing so. If it refused, the business could be taken to court. The FTC also gathered information about the economy and business for Congress and the president.

1918
The U.S. Post Office begins to offer Air Mail service between New York and Washington, D.C.

1919
The United States replaces Europe as the top industrial producer in the world. 43

Economy
1900s

1900s

Union Protection

Before 1900, most women workers in the clothing industry were without legal protection. They often worked seventy hours per week for thirty cents a day. In June 1900, eleven delegates from seven local New York unions came together to create the International Ladies' Garment Workers Union (ILGWU) in order to protect the workers. There were already about 2,000 garment workers represented by the local unions. Most women who initially joined the union were Jewish immigrants working in **sweatshops**. The strength of the union quickly grew. In 1909, the ILGWU fought against the terrible working conditions with a strike in New York City. Thousands of people walked off the job. This action became known as the "Uprising of the 20,000." Another strike in 1910 helped bring about change—the women were given higher wages and overtime pay, as well as safer and more comfortable working conditions. It was the first major settlement between garment companies and the ILGWU. The strikes brought people's attention to the problems and also to the existence and strength of the union.

1901

Billion Dollar Business

In 1901, the sale of the Carnegie Steel Corporation to J.P. Morgan for $492 million made Andrew Carnegie the wealthiest man in the world. The company controlled about one-quarter of the steel and iron production in the U.S. Carnegie retired from business and focused his attention and his fortunes on charity work. Morgan, on the other hand, built on Carnegie's success with the corporation and turned it into U.S. Steel, the first billion-dollar company. To do this, Morgan bought many other large metal companies. U.S. Steel dominated mines, mills, and factories, producing more than 8 billion tons of steel every year. U.S. Steel produced more steel than most countries in the world. In the first year of its sale, U.S. Steel earned $90 million, and it continued to prosper throughout the decade. Looking back, Carnegie realized what a bargain J.P. Morgan had received.

Union Protection

Billion Dollar Business
J. P. Morgan

1900	1901	1904
The price of a six-room house is $3,000.	Oil is discovered in Texas.	Coca-Cola™ becomes the most recognized brand name in the United States.

1901

Stock Scare

In 1901, the New York Stock Exchange suffered a significant loss. Prices fell drastically as stockholders sold, sold, sold. Large railroads bore the brunt of the fall. The Reading, Great Northern, Northern Pacific, and Union Pacific rail lines dropped ten to eleven points. Analysts blamed the crash on banks that needed short-term money and therefore sold stocks. Despite the losses, trading remained steady at 2.2 million shares. The market never reached the level of panic that it experienced in 1907, however, when a rush of selling caused stock prices to plummet. The market suffered the worst single-day drop since 1901. To make matters worse, the 1907 crash came after a long period of falling prices, which businesses blamed on President Roosevelt's attempt to break up trusts. The stock plunge led to a recession in the U.S. that lasted until 1909.

1907

Panic at the Bank

On October 22, 1907, rumors that the banks could collapse caused a rush of people to withdraw their savings. By the end of the day, the Knickerbocker Bank in New York City was out of money. Other banks experienced the same panic, and within a few days, it had spread across the country. The Department of Commerce and Labor, which was established in 1903, was in charge of the nation's economic interests. At the time, banks depended on their own monetary resources. Their stability could be affected by financial difficulties or even rumors. That is what happened in New York City. A drop in copper prices started a crisis. The market for copper mining stocks fell, causing banks with heavy interest in copper to fluctuate. President Roosevelt took action. He sent his secretary of the treasury, George B. Cortelyou, to work with financiers, including J.P. Morgan, to help stabilize the banks. Private bankers also pledged $100 million in gold to save the banks. The government promised that the banks were secure. To make sure of it, Roosevelt placed money in some New York banks that were in trouble. That seemed to ease the panic, but the government did not look into why the panic had happened, nor did it reimburse lost money or put a system in place to prevent another panic in the future. It took until 1913 for the government to improve the banking and monetary systems with the introduction of the Federal Reserve System.

Stock Scare

Panic at the Bank

1907

Leo Baekeland invents the first plastic, which he calls "bakelite."

1908

The Graduate School of Business Administration is founded in Harvard, Massachusetts.

The economy is affected by many factors that create constant changes. For a government to run effectively, it must impose taxes on the people who live in the country. Taxes are used in a variety of ways—from paying the salaries of elected representatives to funding road repairs. To cover the cost of these items, the government taxes income, purchases, and properties, for example. Imagine that you are an economist and you have been hired to help the government fnd a fair way to tax certain items. Based on what you have learned in this book, think about how you would tax items based on where they were made, as well as other factors. Do they pay income or property tax?

Become an Economist

Over the next week, make a list of items that are taxed and at what percentage. Most receipts will include the amount of tax paid on a separate line. How much tax do you pay on food? What percent of sales tax is charged on clothing? When your parents fill up their car with fuel, how much tax do they pay? Talk to an adult, such as a parent or teacher, about the ways they pay taxes. Be sure to use the amount before taxes for your calculation. Next, use a calculator to determine how much tax you would pay on a certain item. For example, if you paid $1.21 in taxes on a restaurant bill for $20.17, divide 20.17 by 1.21 to calculate the tax. On this bill, you paid 0.0599, which rounds to 0.06. Percent means "one per hundred," so 0.06 is equal to 6 percent. Once you have made a list of items, compare the percent of tax paid on each. Are all of the items taxed the same? If not, why do you think they are taxed differently? Is this fair?

FURTHER
Research

Many books and websites provide information about economy. To learn more about this topic, borrow books from the library, or surf the Internet.

Books

Most libraries have computers that connect to a database for researching information. If you input a key word, you will be provided with a list of books in the library that contain information on that topic. Non-fiction books are arranged numerically, using their call number. Fiction books are organized alphabetically by the author's last name.

Websites

For an outline of the U.S. economy, visit **http://usinfo.state.gov/products/pubs/oecon**.

For news about the economy, surf to **www.economist.com**.

Glossary

antitrust: the law against one company controlling an industry

autopsy: the examination of a dead body to determine the cause of death

default: fail to pay back a loan

embargo: stoppage of trade and other commercial activities

Fair Deal: a series of economic and social reforms

Federal Reserve: the U.S. central banking system

fluctuate: rise and fall irregularly

foreclose: to take possession of a property due to the owner not paying the mortgage

generator: a machine that produces power

global warming: the gradual increase in Earth's temperature due to greenhouse gases

Great Depression: an era when the economy was in great decline; beginning in 1929 and lasting through the 1930s

inflation: increase in prices and the fall of money value

lynching: killing someone illegally; usually by hanging

monetarism: control of the supply of money as a way of stabilizing the economy

October War: a war in October 1973 between a group of Arab countries and Israel

recession: an extended period of economic decline

rural electrification: providing homes and businesses in the countryside with electricity

subprime: lending money at a higher rate of interest banks.

sweatshops: places where people work long hours for little pay in poor conditions

vetoed: rejected

Index